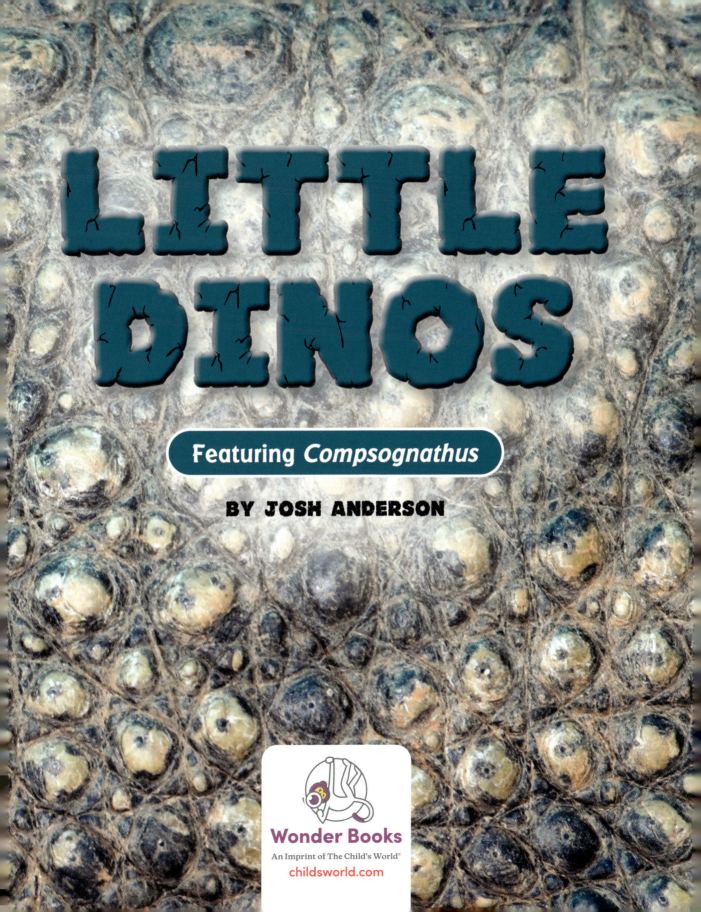

LITTLE DINOS

Featuring *Compsognathus*

BY JOSH ANDERSON

Wonder Books
An Imprint of The Child's World®
childsworld.com

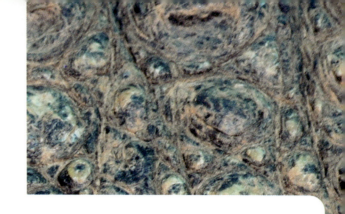

Published by The Child's World®
800-599-READ • www.childsworld.com

Copyright © 2023 by The Child's World®
All rights reserved. No part of this book may be reproduced or utilized in any form or by any means without written permission from the publisher.

Photography Credits
Cover: ©CoreyFord / Getty Images; page 1: ©Pan Xunbin / Shutterstock; page 5: ©Dotted Yeti / Shutterstock; page 6: ©MatthiasKabel / Wikimedia; page 9: ©Elenarts108 / Getty Images; page 10: ©Elenarts108 / Getty Images; page 13: ©DE AGOSTINI PICTURE LIBRARY / Contributor / Getty Images; page 14: ©MR1805 / Getty Images; page 15: ©ullstein bild Dtl. / Contributor / Getty Images; page 16: ©Tuul & Bruno Morandi / Getty Images; page 16: ©Julio Francisco; page 17: ©Julio Francisco; page 19: ©DE AGOSTINI PICTURE LIBRARY / Contributor / Getty Images; page 21: ©JONATHAN NACKSTRAND / Contributor / Getty Images

ISBN Information
9781503865273 (Reinforced Library Binding)
9781503865891 (Portable Document Format)
9781503866737 (Online Multi-user eBook)
9781503867574 (Electronic Publication)

LCCN 2022941012

Printed in the United States of America

About the Author

Josh Anderson has published more than 50 books for children and young adults. His two sons, Leo and Dane, are the greatest joys in his life. Josh's hobbies include coaching youth basketball, no-holds-barred games of Exploding Kittens, reading, and family movie nights. His favorite dinosaur is a secret he'll never share!

CONTENTS

Digging for Bones...4

What We Know...11

Keep Searching...18

Glossary...22
Wonder More...23
Learn More...24
Index...24

CHAPTER 1

Digging for Bones

Pretend you can time travel to a prehistoric age.... You've gone back about 145 million years. You are on a beach in Germany. You see a lizard scurry past your feet. Then another. Suddenly, a small creature darts out of the brush behind you. It runs toward one of the lizards. The creature is about the size of a chicken. It has a long, thin tail. This speedy creature grabs the lizard with a small, three-fingered hand. It puts the lizard in its mouth. Just like that, the tiny lizard is swallowed whole. This creature is *Compsognathus* (komp-sog-NATH-uss), a small **carnivore** of the Late Jurassic Period.

    How do we know so much about a creature who lived long before the first humans walked the Earth? The simple answer: SCIENCE! Let's learn more!

For many years, Compsognathus was the smallest dinosaur ever discovered.

Scientists discovered the bones of a tiny lizard in the stomach of this *Compsognathus* fossil.

Humans have been studying *Compsognathus* for more than 160 years. The first *Compsognathus* **fossils** were found in Germany in 1859. A **paleontologist** named Andreas Wagner studied the **specimen**. At first, he didn't think *Compsognathus* was a dinosaur. This is probably because it was so small. In the years after *Compsognathus* was discovered, similar dinosaurs were found. *Allosaurus* (al-oh-SAWR-uss) and *Ornithomimus* (orr-nith-oh-MY-muss) shared some of the same traits. This led scientists to figure out that *Compsognathus* was indeed a dinosaur.

After *Compsognathus* was identified as a dinosaur, more research was done on the bones. One paleontologist noticed something inside the fossil. It was where the dinosaur's stomach would have been. He thought the object was an **embryo**. Years later, another scientist said the object was too big to be an embryo. It turned out to be the dinosaur's last meal. By identifying what was in its stomach, scientists learned that *Compsognathus* ate lizards.

Many scientists believe that birds **evolved** from dinosaurs. One of the earliest known birds was *Archaeopteryx* (ar-kee-OP-tur-iks). *Compsognathus* had a lot in common with this creature. They both lived in the Late Jurassic Period. And their fossils have been found in similar places. They also shared many of the same features. Both had short bodies with long legs. Both had hollow bones like the birds of today. The similarities helped scientists discover the link between dinosaurs and birds.

Compsognathus may have been small, but it had a mouth full of sharp teeth.

Compsognathus was a fast runner and could easily catch quick-moving lizards.

CHAPTER 2

What We Know

Compsognathus belonged to a group of dinosaurs called theropods. The theropod family includes all meat-eating dinosaurs. Theropods had three toes. They walked on two legs. *Compsognathus's* tail made up more than half the length of its entire body. Many scientists think its body was covered with feathers.

When It Lived: 145 million years ago – The Late Jurassic Period

First Discovered: 1859, Germany

Scientists think *Compsognathus's* long tail helped with balance as it chased **prey**. *Compsognathus* may have also been a scavenger. This means it ate dead animals. But most of its meals likely came from small animals it hunted. *Compsognathus* may have hunted in groups. It was common for a smaller dinosaur to team up with others to hunt larger creatures.

FUN FACTS

- For years, *Compsognathus* was known as the smallest dinosaur. But smaller dinosaurs, like *Microraptor*, have been discovered since then.
- The name *Compsognathus* means "pretty jaw."
- *Compsognathus* was featured in several of the *Jurassic Park* movies.
- Everything we know about *Compsognathus* comes from just two fossils. One was discovered in Germany. The other was found in France.
- *Compsognathus* had large eyes for its small size. This probably meant it had good eyesight.

THEN AND NOW

A second nearly complete *Compsognathus* fossil was found in France in 1971. Researchers thought they'd found a new **species** at first. This specimen was larger than the one found in Germany. They also thought they were looking at a dinosaur that had flippers instead of fingers. They figured out later that the flipper was actually a front claw. The size difference between the two samples was explained later as well. The *Compsognathus* found in Germany was probably a young dinosaur. The one in France was a full-grown adult.

There has been a lot of debate about what kind of hands Compsognathus had.

Microraptor was about the size of a pigeon.

Compsognathus wasn't the only tiny dinosaur. Here are a couple of other small but mighty dinos from the ancient world.

Microraptor (MYK-row-rahp-tur) had four wings and may have been able to fly. It lived about 20 million years after *Compsognathus*. Its fossils have been found in China.

Saltopus (SAHL-tuh-puss) lived millions of years earlier than *Compsognathus*. *Saltopus* was only about 8 inches (20 centimeters) tall and likely ate insects. It had five fingers on each of its hands.

UP FOR DEBATE

Both existing *Compsognathus* fossils are very well preserved and mostly complete. This means paleontologists have a very good idea of what the dino looked like—except for its hands. There is still no clear answer on whether *Compsognathus* had two, three, or even four fingers on each hand. The earliest drawing from 1861 showed *Compsognathus* with three fingers. But even the discovery of a second complete *Compsognathus* fossil didn't settle the issue.

COMPSOGNATHUS
(komp-sog-NATH-uss) VS

Length: 2 feet (61 cm)

Weight: 7 pounds (3.2 kilograms)

Top Speed: 40 miles (64 kilometers) per hour

Weakness: Small size, but it may have been the top predator in the places it lived

Best Defense or Weapon: Speedy and flexible; had sharp, curved teeth

AQUILOPS
(AH-kwill-ops)

Length: 2 feet (61 cm)

Weight: 3.3 pounds (1.5 kg)

Top Speed: unknown

Weakness: This tiny *Triceratops* relative probably wasn't as fast as small theropods like *Compsognathus*

Best Defense or Weapon: Sharp horns on the side of its head

CHAPTER 3

Keep Searching

New dinos are found each year. In 2021, 42 new kinds of dinosaurs were discovered. But sometimes scientists think they've discovered a dinosaur when they actually haven't.

In 2020, a group of paleontologists wrote about a tiny skull found inside a piece of ancient **amber**. They believed the skull belonged to a very tiny dinosaur. It was just half an inch (1.3 cm) long. It was smaller than a hummingbird. Scientists named it *Oculudentavis* (ock–yoo–loo–den–TAY–vuss).

But then, another *Oculudentavis* fossil was discovered. It was the creature's whole body. Scientists noticed that its teeth were attached directly to its jawbone. But dinosaur teeth are found in holes inside the mouth called sockets. The creature also had lizard eyes and shoulder bones. It turned out that *Oculudentavis* was actually a lizard, not a dinosaur.

Many amazing prehistoric specimens have been found preserved in amber.

One dinosaur discovery of 2021 answered a question scientists have had for a long time. Scientists knew that some dinosaurs spent time in a cold part of Earth called the Arctic Circle. But no one knew if dinosaurs lived there all year long or not. They wondered if dinosaurs **migrated** south in the colder months, like birds do. A recent discovery of tiny bones from dinosaur babies may have settled the question. Dinosaurs were nesting and giving birth in the Arctic Circle. That means they probably lived in the Arctic year-round.

What will we learn next? And how will it change what we know about *Compsognathus* and other dinosaurs? Who will make these amazing discoveries? It could be YOU!

Dinosaur fossils have been found on every continent, including frozen Antarctica.

GLOSSARY

amber (AM-burr): a hard, yellowish, and often see-through substance that formed from a thick fluid that oozes from some trees called resin. The resin that formed amber came from trees that grew millions of years ago.

carnivore (KAR-nih-vor): an animal that eats the flesh of another animal

embryo (EM-bree-yoh): an animal or plant that is just starting to develop. An embryo grows inside an egg, a seed, or its mother.

evolved (eh-VALVD): developed over a long time

fossil (FAH-sul): the remains or traces of plants and animals that lived long ago

migrate (MY-grayt): to move from one region to another

paleontologist (pay-lee-on-TOL-uh-jist): a scientist who studies animal and plant fossils for information about life in the past

prehistoric (pree-hiss-TORE-ick): belonging to a period in a time before written history

prey (PRAY): an animal that is hunted or killed by another animal for food

species (SPEE-sheez): a group of living things that are able to reproduce

specimen (SPEH-seh-mehn): material used in testing, examination, or study

WONDER MORE

Think About It: What would you do if you were suddenly much smaller than everyone around you? How would it change your life if you were the size of *Compsognathus*?

Talk About It: Ask your family or friends about a time in their life when they wished they were bigger or smaller. Can you think of a time when you wished you were a different size? Share that as part of the conversation.

Write About It: Imagine you could run 40 miles (64 km) per hour like *Compsognathus*. That's about five times faster than the average human. How would your life be different? What would you do with your amazing speed?

MESOZOIC ERA

Triassic Period	Jurassic Period	Cretaceous Period
201–252 Million Years Ago	145–201 Million Years Ago	66–145 Million Years Ago

LEARN MORE

BOOKS

Blazing, George, et al. *Dinosaur Encyclopedia for Kids: The Big Book of Prehistoric Creatures*. Emeryville, CA: Rockridge Press, 2021.

Daniels, Patricia. *1,000 Facts About Dinosaurs, Fossils, and Prehistoric Life*. Washington, DC: National Geographic Kids, 2020.

Kelly, Erin Suzanne. *Dinosaurs*. New York: Children's Press, 2021.

WEBSITES

Visit our website for links about *Compsognathus*: **childsworld.com/links**

Note to Parents, Caregivers, Teachers, and Librarians: We routinely verify our web links to make sure they are safe and active sites. So encourage your readers to check them out!

INDEX

Allosaurus, 7
Aquilops, 17
Archaeopteryx, 8
Arctic Circle, 20

bones, 6, 8, 18, 20

France, 12–13

Germany, 4, 7, 11–13

Jurassic Park, 12
Jurassic Period, 4, 8, 11

Microraptor, 12, 14–15

Oculudentavis, 18

Ornithomimus, 7

Saltopus, 15

theropods, 11, 17

Wagner, Andreas, 7